Foreword by Peter N. Vacca

The
SEED
Of FAITH

Living The Now Word Of God

PAMELA A. SEGNERI

The Seed Of Faith - Living The Now Word Of God

Copyright © 2021 - Pamela Segneri

All rights reserved. This book is protected by the copyright laws of Australia. This book may not be copied or reprinted for commercial gain or profit. The use of short quotations or occasional page copying for personal or group study is permitted and encouraged provided the source is acknowledged. Permission will be granted upon request. Unless otherwise identified, Scripture quotations are taken from the New American Standard Bible® NASB® Copyright © 1960, 1971, 1977, 1995, 2020 by The Lockman Foundation. Used by permission. All rights reserved. www.Lockman.org. Scripture quotations marked TPT are from The Passion Translation®. Copyright © 2017 by BroadStreet Publishing® Group, LLC. Used by permission. All rights reserved. thePassionTranslation.com. Scripture quotations marked NKJV are from The Holy Bible, New King James Version. Copyright © 1982 by Thomas Nelson, Inc. Used by permission. All rights reserved. www.thenkjvbible.com. Emphasis with Scripture quotations is the author's own. Please note that Mountain Train Media's publishing style capitalizes certain pronouns in Scripture that refer to the Father, Son, and Holy Spirit, and may differ from some Bible publishers' styles. Take note that the name satan and related names are not capitalized. We choose not to acknowledge him, even to the point of violating grammatical rules.

Published by Mountain Train Media
QLD, Australia
publishing@mountaintrainmedia.com.au
www.mountaintrainmedia.com.au

ISBN: 978-0-6453782-0-7

Dedication

It would be remiss to not firstly dedicate this book to Our Lord Jesus Christ, for without Him there is nothing to write.

To my husband Paul always encouraging and believing in me when the going was tough.

Especially dedicated to my sons Simon and Todd. They are extraordinary young men of God who had the 'Seed Of Faith' planted in them as babies.

Finally, yet incredibly importantly - to my parents, my grand-parents and my great grand-parents. Without whom the 'Seed Of Faith' legacy may not have been planted.

Acknowledgements

As with any project there have been many who have encouraged and assisted along the way.

I want to especially acknowledge the tireless work of my husband Paul, his editing and design skills have been a gift.

To my dear friends who took the time to endorse this work.

Peter and Pattie Vacca, Bruce and Cheryl Lindley, Adam F. Thompson, Phillip and Lorelee Colley, Daniel Duval and Darren Canning. I appreciate you all so much not simply for the endorsements but for all you bring to my life.

To my friends Robyn Martin, Lynn Johnston and Linda Rohrbaugh. Thank you for your love and encouragement along the way.

Contents

Foreword: Peter N. Vacca....p9

Endorsements....p11

Introduction....p17

Chapter 1: What Is This Thing Called Faith?....p21

Chapter 2: The Substance Of Things Hoped For....p33

Chapter 3: Get A Vision....p41

Chapter 4: Mustard Seed Faith....p47

Chapter 5: In The Name Of Jesus....p53

Chapter 6: Fear Or Faith In The Face Of Fire....p59

Chapter 7: Which Faith?....p65

Chapter 8: The Gift Of Faith....p71

Chapter 9: Faith And The Seer....p77

Chapter 10: Promises Received....p81

Chapter 11: It Is Finished....p87

Chapter 12: Jack....p95

Chapter 13: Faith In Action....p101

Chapter 14: What To Do When Faith Seems Weak?....p111

8   THE SEED OF FAITH

Foreword

Having known Pamela and her family over many decades, I know this book is an expression of her faith. After teaching her in Bible College in the early 1990's, she later ministered along side me, especially during the healing meetings where her faith was demonstrated in very real and practical ways.

I am very impressed and inspired by Pamela's articulated exposition of this awesome and challenging presentation on ***The Seed of Faith - Living the Now Word of God***.

I personally found it to be inspiring, well balanced and very encouraging. I believe this has the ability to open up new era horizons of revelation knowledge, prompting the reader to an expectation for bigger and better faith living.

I consider this to indeed be a very special and timely book that will make a good read and will encourage you mightily.

I encourage you to rediscover 'The Seed of Faith' within you.

Peter N. Vacca

Apostle & Founder

Bethesda Ministries International

Endorsements

The following endorsements have been made by men and women of God who have known Pamela for many years and who in their own right, have strong ministries throughout the world today. Reading these endorsements will encourage you in rediscovering your Seed of Faith.

The Seed of Faith - Living The Now Word Of God is much more than a book on faith. It will change your way of living! How can I be so sure? It has done that for Pamela Segneri.

Her understanding of the realm of faith and her ability to trust God in the NOW no matter what will impact you. Everything that you read here, she lives. It won't be long until you are experiencing that as well.

As Pamela shares, the essence of the faith life is to understand that 'The seed of faith is IN us' and you can live your faith in everyday life.

As you read about Pamela's own walk of faith, you will discover this part of God's heart for you too! Because one of the things I love most about Pamela is that she freely helps others learn & live what she has experienced. And then you will begin to freely do that for others too!

So get ready for your faith to be inspired and grow!

Bruce & Cheryl Lindley

Founding Apostle - ARC Global Apostolic Community

International Apostle - Harvest International Ministries Apostolic Network

www.arcglobal.org

Pamela is a woman of faith who lives her message. She has used her faith to navigate mountains and valleys and has come through shining.

This book will provide you with a Biblical and practical approach to a faith walk that will produce real fruit. She has paired personal experience and practical application with the Word of God to encourage, motivate, and strengthen your faith.

If you are looking to be emboldened in your faith walk, this is a right now word for you!

Daniel Duval
Bride Ministries International

www.bridemovement.com

Have you ever read a book that truly inspires your faith? Well, *The Seed Of Faith - Living The Now Word Of God* by Pamela Segneri is that book!

It is a clear, solid and powerful work filled with revelation that will ignite your hunger for God. I love this book and I deeply respect and honour its author.

Adam F. Thompson

Prophetic Ministry and International Author

www.voiceoffireministries.org

I'm so excited about the contents of this book. It is like a sword that brings life to those that read it.

This message is a very timely prophetic message, yet it is a Timeless message. I love the way Pamela reveals the practical understanding and reality of day to day Faith. This is a very easy book to read, yet unpacks the word of God thoroughly.

Lorellee Colley

Director - Destiny Strategies

www.destinystrategies.com.au

Some of my favorite books I have read are on faith. Faith is the substance of things hoped for and the evidence of things unseen. When I was 18 years old, I went to Bible School and Paul Yonggi Cho from South Korea's largest charismatic church came to preach on faith. I was young but still remember that sermon. I realised that the Christian life was founded, built and prospered because of faith and I wanted to have faith. I believe that I have obtained the life of faith.

I pray that this book strengthens you. Pamela is a wonderful woman of God who I met many years ago now on her TV show. She has been a blessing to so many in the Kingdom and I know that as you read this book you are going to be inspired to take greater leaps of faith.

Darren Canning
Revivalist and Author
www.darrencanning.tv

16 THE SEED OF FAITH

Introduction

Faith is perhaps the simplest and most difficult discipline we ever have to master. So this may be the shortest or most protracted book ever. I am aiming for something in the middle of those two extremes.

Always consider who is the loudest voice in your head. For us it should be the voice of God.

'When your soul is full, you turn down even the sweetest honey. But when your soul is starving, every bitter thing becomes sweet.' Proverbs 27:7 (TPT)

We must be careful not to fill up with other voices and opinions because if we do the sweet revelation word will be rejected.

'Faith', in that word is our anchor so we do not get swept away by any wind of opinion or doctrine. Always remembering that it is our faith in the Lord Jesus Christ that is our strong tower. That is our anchor!

Make no mistake there is a very real war raging in the heavenlies (spirit realm). We cannot be passive observers, we must be active participants. The body of

Christ is on a war footing. Remembering always the battle is the Lords and He has already won the victory. So this is when we assemble on the already drawn battle lines, lift our shields of Faith and stand!

I love that old saying, "from little acorns great oak trees grow". Those acorns are a metaphorical representation of our seed of faith. From those humble seed beginnings we grow and become all that we can be in God. Everything He wrote on our scroll, everything He predestined for each and every one of us starts with that tiny seed of faith.

Isaiah 61:3 says that we become the **Mighty** oaks of righteousness, the planting of the Lord. *(emphasis is mine)*

This is who we can be… starting from that tiny seed, planted in good soil, given the sunlight and nurture required and watered carefully and regularly. One of the important things to remember is that this is a life, a walk of faith, it is a lifestyle which requires discipline, there's that word most don't like. To my mind it is not a negative.

Consider this, "I am a disciple of the Lord Jesus Christ so I desire to be disciplined in my lifestyle and choices". Those right choices are manifested in the development of the seed and how we nurture those seeds determine the outcomes in our lives.

This is written to inspire and encourage.

The Seed of Faith…. it is in us!

CHAPTER 1

What Is This Thing Called Faith?

This is a very serious question, as we all know there have been many phrases coined in regard to faith. Let me say negativity destroys faith, so our attitude, not only to this subject but to life in general is incredibly important. So whilst I am not ignorant of the negative phrases that have been coined in relation to Faith, I choose not to give them any credence in my life or in this text.

I woke the other morning with this…..

When every part of you is screaming this is impossible, yet there is a word from heaven, a word quickened by Holy Spirit that is there and you can't ignore it………. That's Faith! When the world around you is closing in and yelling that you are wrong, it can't happen.... And yet you stand firm.... That's Faith!

Remember Nehemiah, he had a word from God to rebuild the walls of Jerusalem. In the natural everything was against him, impossible even — but God. Nehemiah had a major roadblock in that he was in the employ of the King in a different nation. Not only did God make a way, He orchestrated that the King would give Nehemiah letters of passage and requests of provision. This was a big thing that God had called him to accomplish. Once he arrived in Jerusalem and inspected the walls, again in the natural it wasn't good. But Nehemiah had the word of faith.

Holy Spirit is there with the word so you can reach out and seize it and don't let go...... That's Faith!

Let those words be your anchor throughout life. They of course can be as profound or perfunctory in our world as we choose.

I pray they will be profound and life changing, course correcting, allowing us to fulfil our God designed destiny.

Seems to me we are only beginning to scratch the surface of something that is such an important part of the life of a believer.

'And without faith living within us it would be impossible to please God....' Hebrews 11:6 (TPT)

Now look at the rest of that verse

'For we come to God in faith knowing that he is real and that he rewards the faith of those who passionately seek him.'

We must believe that He firstly is, and then that He rewards us for seeking Him. To believe those two things we must have the most basic faith, salvation faith through the grace of heaven.

We all surely have a desire to please God, if not - then the words of those great Pentecostal evangelists 'we are only buying fire insurance' are probably appropriate.

We all want to hear the words from the throne, 'Well done good and faithful now enter your rest', except that is a misquote. It actually reads,

'....enter into the joy of your master/lord.' Matthew 25:21,23 *(NASB and NKJV).*

The reason I point this out is because it occurs to me that entering the joy of our Lord is quite different to entering your rest. This parable infers there is more to be done as we partner with Him. Whereas rest would imply there is no more for us to do, our work here is finished at least for the present. Let me underline that our work is not toil, the curse of toil was broken at the cross.

I am pointing out the difference because too often it is easier to do nothing, after all God said rest. I believe we are in the rest of God and perhaps we are only just beginning to grasp that truth. What I understand from this scripture in Matthew 25:21,23 is the battle has been won, the toil is finished so the work and warfare we partake in has an ease about it. That will always bring joy as we achieve with the Lord.

Please be aware believing that God exists, is not the same as believing the devil doesn't. It is a similar conundrum to the age old discussion that the absence of war is peace. Simply not true, that's just a ceasefire, tenuous at best. So to plainly state it, just because someone doesn't believe the devil exists, we cannot draw the conclusion that God does. Atheists do not believe there is a devil or God. We and every other living soul in order to enter the kingdom and reap the benefits therein must believe that God is!

He is the Alpha and Omega, the first and the last so in order to bear witness to Hebrews 11:6 we must discover Him for ourselves to believe He is!

I do want to please my Heavenly Father so I endeavour to run the race that is set before me.

> 'Not that I have already attained, or am already perfected; but I press on, that I may lay hold of that for which Christ Jesus has also laid hold

of me. Bretheren, I do not count myself to have apprehended; but one thing I do, forgetting those things which are behind and reaching forward to those things which are ahead, I press toward the goal for the prize of the upward call of God in Christ Jesus.' Philippians 3:12-16 (NKJV)

We do that by faith - there is no other way!

It would be so good if I had a dollar for every time someone told me emphatically they had faith and not just regular faith but huge mountain obliterating faith, yet their lives don't reflect that truth. It is not about people experiencing difficult circumstances, it is our reactions or responses to those circumstances.

How do we act in tragic or challenging situations? As people of faith we must keep our eyes firmly set on Christ and that seed of faith growing within us which sets us apart and encourages us that we are passing through the situation. We are not locked in to the current circumstance.

*'Even though I walk **through** the valley of the shadow of death, I fear no evil, for You are with me; Your rod and Your staff, they comfort me.' Psalms 23:4* (NASB) *(emphasis is mine)*

When we are in difficult places, we are going through — that should be our automatic response, almost a reflex action if you like. That's the Faith situation report.

Those who know me well know I am not a camper, so when I read Psalms 23:4, I see that Holy Spirit is not a camper. He is going through and I am going with Him. We are pioneers often traversing new and uncharted territory and we carefully plant our homesteads or outposts in the midst of unfavourable territory. When the seed of faith is planted within your Spirit things change, we change.

There is an old saying which refers to many things not just faith that says; 'If you've got it you don't need to advertise it.' My Mum used to have a fridge magnet that read 'Who you are speaks so loudly I can't hear a word you are saying'. That should cause pause for consideration.

So really it doesn't matter what comes out of our mouth if it doesn't line up with how we live. Why? Because we have changed!

Let me temper that, of course there are faith statements and decrees and in terms of those things, we may not be there yet. However we are calling things that be not as though they are (See Romans 4:17b). An important note: we are to call into being that which does not exist. Not to call things that are as though they do not exist. We are calling heaven to earth.

This is an incredibly simple differentiation and

I know there is a school of thought that will say it doesn't matter. However, I would propose that it does make a difference otherwise why would the infallible Word of God put it that way?

Faith can see further, our faith in The Lord Jesus Christ will allow us to see outcomes that our natural selves cannot imagine. Faith can see around corners, and through mountains. The beautiful thing about God's design is that all things truly work together for good and I see that the giftings and callings of God work together to bring the optimum outcome. I will talk about that more in a later chapter.

When we operate in Faith we are aware of the circumstance but we see into the future. That is due to the word of faith and as we speak it out we are drawn towards it. I believe our Faith is the cord that pulls the manifestation of our prayers into our reality. So for instance in the case of a sickness or disease we don't tell it to go, we speak healing, restoration, resurrection power by faith and it must go. It may go instantaneously which is always great or it may take a little time for the receiver to come into line with the faith we are releasing. In those cases we stand firm — do not allow anyone to change your faith confession.

> *'Therefore, take up the full armor of God, so that you will be able to resist in the evil day, and*

having done everything, to stand firm.' Ephesians 6:13 (NASB1995)

Today we still need the full armour of God, we put it on by faith. We still need the power of the blood of Jesus and we receive that by faith.

The Kingdom of God is all about and only about faith!

I love the story of Peter and John in Acts 3 at the Gate Beautiful. The man they encountered had been lame/crippled from birth. Now that according to most peoples reality is a life sentence of begging or in todays terms, being on a disability pension or benefit. In any situation it is living a lesser life. Peter grasped the man's hand and in the name of Jesus Christ, (the authority that he and we can all operate in) commanded him to stand up and walk. In the NASB it reads: 'he seized him and power flowed through him.' So there were two things in operation — the word wrapped in faith and Holy Spirit Gift of Healings.

None of the tools we have been given need to work in isolation, in fact they are probably most powerful as they operate in concert. It is also so important to remember everything in the Kingdom operates by faith starting with salvation. Every step of our walk as a believer must be undergirded with Faith in the one true Living God.

We are saved by Faith through Grace. The Grace of heaven is upon us to open the way for our salvation. That's when faith must kick in, faith to believe it happened.

Faith is about a promise from God, whether a scripture that has been quickened to us or a word of prophecy we've received. Perhaps a dream or vision we've personally received. These are the seeds of promise, seeds of faith to call those things into being.

In the New Testament our word for Faith is translated from the Greek word *pistis*. I include the Strong's definition: credence; moral conviction, (of religious truth, or the truthfulness of God or a religious teacher), especially reliance upon Christ for salvation; abstractly, constancy in profession; by extension, the system of religious belief (Gospel) truth itself; assurance, belief, believe, faith, fidelity.

Our reliance on Christ - that really pins it down for me. The word and the concept of Faith often seems quite ambiguous and we need to break it down so we can understand it and apply it in our everyday life. It is our assurance that what Jesus the Living Word said is true and He will do it. He is doing it.

In fact as we understand God's time (Kairos) as opposed to our time (Chronos) which is linear, Chronos has a beginning, a middle and an end. Kairos is not like that. Simply put, in the Spirit realm things are quite fluid and can and do move up and down and fold back on itself in the timeline. I say all that to say what Jesus said has already happened - Every victory already won! We just have to agree by faith and keep on agreeing until it manifests. Thats the constancy in profession that Strong spoke of, that regardless of how things may look we keep our eyes on that seed of Faith. As we do that we will come through the circumstance or situation.

It is necessary to add, Holy Spirit doesn't always use the A to B route. I would encourage you not to lose heart when it doesn't seem to be working out as you thought it would. Many times God is touching and healing things which to us may have been irrelevant or unimportant to the subject at hand, yet God has a talent for weaving all things together beautifully.

Trust God no matter what! It is a simple enough statement and I believe we all set out endeavouring to live that way. Then life happens. At that moment when things are not perfect - that is when you learn to trust, have faith and believe God no matter what.

It is a journey, it's not a season or era. It is over all those time frames, it is your life.

'.... *However, when the Son of Man comes, will He find faith on the earth?*' *Luke 18:8b* (NASB)

The context of that verse is urging us to continue praying and continue expecting just like the persistent widow with the judge. God is the righteous judge and He will bring swift justice to those who do not show mercy to those who are trusting in Him.

CHAPTER 2

The Substance Of Things Hoped For

'Now faith is the substance of things hoped for, the evidence of things not seen.' Hebrews 11:1
(NKJV)

We know that word and we all love it. I guess we love the hope that it sparks within each one of us, the hope that God hears us and is with us and there are better days to come.

So how do we establish these things into our reality?

In the NASB, Hebrews 11:1 reads Faith is the assurance or certainty, in the NKJV it reads substance.

The Passion translation puts it simply,

> 'Now faith brings our hopes into reality and becomes the foundation needed to acquire the things we long for. It is all the evidence required to prove what is still unseen.' Hebrews 11:1 (TPT)

We see that and get excited. We then pray for something and get disappointed when what we prayed for doesn't materialise.

Disappointment is insidious and pervades every part of our conscious, unconscious and subconsciousness if we do not take action and stand against it. I do not believe you can consistently pray in faith if you are disappointed. Now I can hear people protesting that they are not disappointed with God, only that the prayer request wasn't granted. So I would ask why are you then disappointed?

This is such a big issue.

1 John 5:14-15 says something that will transform our belief system as we renew our minds.

> 'This is the confidence which we have before Him, that, if we ask **anything** according to His will, He hears us. And if we know that He hears us in whatever we ask, we know that we have the requests which we have asked from Him.' 1 John 5:14-15 (NASB) (emphasis is mine)

Okay, so looking at that scripture we clearly must

know the will of the Father or at least what His will isn't. So if we know our request is according to His will we should have confidence to boldly come before Him. I guess we have all heard truly heart felt prayers that kind of go "if you will Lord". I am sorry to say they are not faith prayers that stir the heart of God.

So what is it that stirs God's heart? They are the prayers when we get revelation of His Word and we pray it back to Him, thus becoming the voice of His Word (Psalms 103:20). We are all surrounded by angels who are waiting to obey His Word through our voice. Not our word with "in Jesus Name" tacked on as a tag line.

In Revelation 12:11 it reads

'And they overcame him because of the blood of the Lamb and because of the word of their testimony...' (NASB)

The power in that word is when we have our new operating system fully functioning. Our testimony is the Word and the Word is our testimony. We, without Christ cannot overcome him. It is The Blood of Christ and the Word of God, which is Christ and we activate them by faith.

Let's look at Hebrews 11:3

'By faith we understand that the worlds were

prepared by the word of God, so that what is seen was not made out of things which are visible.' (NASB1995)

In other versions of the Bible they used the word framed or created rather than prepared. They both give us very clear pictures of God speaking everything into being. I know we are on the threshold of a time when we the body of Christ, not just a few superstars will do that too. Our words create our reality both good and bad. God was preparing what our world was to be by His Word.

Let's go back to the beginning. This is the Genesis 1 account. In the beginning,

- God said (v3)
- God called (v5)
- God said (v6)
- God called (v8)
- God said (v9)
- God called (v10)
- God said (v11)
- God said (v14)
- God said (v20)

- God blessed them (v22)
- God said (v24)
- God said (v26)
- God blessed them (v28)

God at the very origin of creation is setting out a pattern for us — we get to say and create. We are made in His image, the Godhead (Father, Son and Hoy Spirit) agreed that we should be made in their image. It wasn't that they were short on creative ideas, it was very specific. I personally believe it was the desire of God that we would reflect all three parts of the Godhead - Father, Son and Holy Spirit. We are also a three part being - Spirit, Soul and Body.

Man was told to be fruitful and multiply (Genesis 1:28), when you are fruitful things are being created. In Genesis 2:19 God brought every living creature to man, for him to name them. Right there, God was encouraging Adam to speak creatively. Every time a name is spoken over someone or something it defines their purpose. The names we call people and objects are therefore far more significant than has often been appreciated. In fact, I believe we can and must go further than names, it is the power of the spoken word good or bad. What we have today is what was spoken into being in our yesterdays.

'So faith comes from hearing, and hearing by the word of Christ.' Romans 10:17 (NASB)

We can underline this a little more as we look at the following two scriptures:

'And Jesus answered and said to them, "Truly I say to you, if you have faith and do not doubt, you will not only do what was done to the fig tree, but even if you say to this mountain, 'Be taken up and cast into the sea,' it will happen. And whatever you ask in prayer, believing, you will receive it all."' Matthew 21:21-22 (NASB)

'And Jesus answered saying to them, "Have faith in God. Truly I say to you, whoever says to this mountain, 'Be taken up and thrown into the sea,' and does not doubt in his heart, but believes that what he says is going to happen, it will be granted him.' Mark 11:22-23 (NASB)

You will have what you say. It does not say you will only have the good faith filled confessions! We must discipline our tongues by first disciplining our minds. Renewing our minds daily with the Word of God.

We will have what we say (Proverbs 13:2-3), let's take up that challenge not from me but from heaven. We have at this moment in history the ability to reframe our world, as we apply the seed of faith that the Lord has sown into us. I would caution that we not become reckless, then disillusioned because what we wanted didn't happen. Jesus said He only did what He saw the Father doing. There is such a powerful message in that. The timing of God is not necessarily our timing, sometimes the answer is wait! If the answer is wait it is not because God is too busy to get to us. Often times it's because there are other things God wants to establish in our lives and then give us the answer we asked for.

There are many things in the Word because of the covenant we have through Jesus that we can already pray with confidence — for instance healing, deliverance, salvation and prosperity. These were established by Christ however, we must make sure we understand what each really means not just what we thought they meant.

Then take up the sword of the spirit which is the Word of God and wield it with confidence. As we do that by faith, knowing that no word of His returns to Him void — it always accomplishes what it is sent forth to do — everything changes.

Lets create the substance in our own world, people are watching……

CHAPTER 3

Get A Vision

Yes, I said it! Vision is incredibly important as we move through this lifestyle of Faith in Christ.

Many people have said and in fact continue to say that vision is New Age, imagination is New Age, so what do I say to that. Yes, yes it is the New and Glorious Age of the Church as we arise and shine and reclaim the tools which were laid down due to fear. God created these things for our benefit, other groups have simply adopted them as they fell into obscurity within the church.

I believe God Himself has vision for everything He creates before He creates it. Since, as we have already agreed we are made His image and likeness, it is judicious to believe we too should have a vision of what we are speaking into being. Then as we read in John, He is in us as we are in Him, is it not reasonable to believe that His attributes are in us?

Let's consider for a moment our natural parents. We carry within us portions of their DNA. Go to any doctor and the first thing they ask is about any inherited defects. What medical history did they inadvertently pass on to you.

Now as Born Again believers we have by definition had New Birth and now recognise we are first Spirit beings. This is where we zoom right past the edge of reason into the realm of the miraculous, the realm of heavenly realities.

We have the opportunity to embrace our God given birthright by Faith.

So what does that mean?

Simply put, we need to see it! We must have the vision for whatever we are believing for. Let's put our sanctified imaginations to work. We can build a new life with that vision.

A word of caution here, that does not mean I am advocating dumping your current life. Many of us have seen families destroyed because of a lack of understanding. I do not believe there is cause to fear your imagination if what you are believing for is in line with the Word. It is the same with our prayers, if they are not in line with the Word of God then what we are praying is out of order.

One of my favourite passages of scripture is Psalms 37:4

> *'Delight yourself in the Lord; And He will give you the desires of your heart.'* (NASB)

This is a safeguard, not an opportunity to blab it and grab it!

As we delight in the Lord, as we are soft and tender toward Him, as we gaze upon Him with great love not once but always, this is the present continuous tense so it is ongoing - it is a complete lifestyle change. He becomes the centre of our being and as we do this some interesting things begin to happen - things that were difficult to establish previously become established.

I want to unpack this, Romans 12:2 is a scripture we all know on one level or another. I am interested to hear people quote this and often times only quote part of the verse. Which reads 'be transformed by the renewing of your mind'.

That is not enough! We must read and believe from the beginning of the verse

'And do not be conformed to this world, but be transformed by the renewing of your mind,...'

And then the end of the verse

'...so that you may prove what the will of God is, that which is good and acceptable and perfect.'
Romans 12:2 (NASB)

When you stitch all three parts together you get the context and therefore the answer.

When we delight ourselves in the Lord we are not conforming to the world, because it makes no sense to the world.

This allows us to receive the Word which we are reading and consequently change our minds. This is effectually like loading a new operating system so in times of stress or trouble we default to this new system of thought - God's thoughts for and about us and our lives.

The third part ensures that as long as we do the first two parts we are protected in the will of God. So anything we are believing for, getting a vision for, at this point ensuring it is not us off on a carnal tangent, it is us in the place we were born to be.

The realm of the Spirit is seeing, hearing and believing heavenly miraculous realities - that is where we must live and as we plant our seed of Faith here we are attaching an invisible cord of Faith by which we bring those miracles of heaven into the here and now.

CHAPTER 4

Mustard Seed Faith

When I was a very young child going to Sunday school and listening in awe to the exciting and incredible Bible stories, I let my imagination take me to those places and events - they were real to me not simply words on a page. I understood something of the present continuous nature of Spiritual truths - in other words this was not a history lesson to me.

The pages of the Bible were filled with love, hate, joy, despair, victory and defeat - everything that effects the human condition. The one thing that permeated my being as I immersed myself in those pages was Faith. I didn't realise it at the time, probably because as a child I had no vocabulary for that.

I took the words as truth. I didn't need an explanation to talk me into it (or out of it) I just believed. If God had said it then I believed it!

What was happening even at a very early age was Holy Spirit was planting seeds of Faith. At that time all I understood was I knew things with a conviction. That belief was not from anything I had learned in the natural sense but was from something much more compelling.

Those seeds of faith have grown over a lifetime, I pray they will continue to grow and bear fruit because we are not finished yet!

That brings me to the mustard seed, a tiny seed with a big future. When we look at this plant they have a spreading, multi stemmed growth habit with a drooping or weeping branch structure. That could be a picture of our lives well lived. Multi stemmed because we are called to have influence in many areas. The drooping or weeping structure speaks to me of protection from the elements and compassion.

I love that Jesus uses the mustard seed illustration in Luke 17 in response to the apostles asking Him to increase their faith. The seed germinates quite quickly, 8-10 days under the proper conditions. We'll put a pin in that as we're coming back to it later.

The mustard plant is not a tree as it is a herb, so technically it's a shrub. It is very fast growing, in 12 weeks it's a fully formed shrub which depending on the variety will grow between 2 and 6.5 metres - exceptional plants can reach 10 metres in ideal conditions. They have a multi stemmed growth habit and can have up to a 6.5 metre spread.

They are significant plants. Jesus sees that potential in a tiny mustard seed just as He sees that potential in our Faith. Like the mustard plant, to grow our faith well we must have the right conditions.

What are the ideal conditions for faith growth?

1. Start with the Word of God (the seed)

2. Water with the Holy Spirit

3. Let the sun of righteousness shine (our relationship with Jesus)

4. Continue to feed with the Word of God

If your desire is to increase your faith, it is wise to increase your desire for the Word of God. There is no right or wrong way to read the Bible. We're only wrong if we don't do it!

It is our food and daily we can access fresh manna. Holy Spirit will reveal truths to us and this is a very exciting daily pursuit. Sometimes you may start to read a portion of scripture and something, a word or a theme captures your attention or imagination. Then as you go with it, following where the Holy Spirit is leading, He may be desiring to lead you onto a new path which will lead you to your destiny. We must always remain open to His leading so that our seed of faith may have the optimum conditions for growth.

If you don't seem to get those leadings don't be concerned. Before you start to read the Word it may help to worship for a while. Not just singing songs but rather pouring out your heart of love to the Father. That often helps to get us to the place we need to start from. Also it is helpful to invite Holy Spirit into this time, ask Him to guide you and He will.

Never fall prey to self condemnation because your devotion to the Lord is not like someone else's. Our journey through life with the Lord is not a competition and it is most certainly not a sprint. We are in it for the long haul so it is important that our spiritual stamina is maintained.

Pray in tongues, fast and share communion. These are all very important and one more thing - be in relationship with others. This helps our balance. Find people who are further along than you are, perhaps they are operating in a realm you desire to. Allow a relationship to build and allow them to speak into your life. That is what the body is called to do, discipleship.

Don't stress if you currently don't have those

people in your life. Trust God, have faith and He will bring the right ones along at the right time.

Remember they are not adopting you, sometimes we may only journey together for a short while - others are for a lifetime. Often times it may be for a specific undertaking. In all these things let your faith grow knowing God always works all things together for good.

CHAPTER 5

In The Name Of Jesus

I often listen to people pray and hear "in the name of Jesus" as a tag line. Sort of like abracadabra, done - poof, and something mystical and unexpected happens.

I know that the name of Jesus is all powerful and at His name demons tremble, yet that's not what I am hearing. Jesus Himself said to His disciples in six references in the Gospel of John chapter 14 through 16, whatever you ask in my name. Ask in My Name, we have been taught to pray that way and it is absolutely correct. Let me ask how many times have you prayed and said "in the Name of Jesus" and nothing happened.

In light of the importance of the faith truth, I believe our prayer strategies could stand another look.

Please understand this is not a judgement and I would like it to be a clarification bringing inspiration. As we read the scriptures we are getting to know Jesus the Living Word. He is the bridegroom we are preparing for. The more we know Him, the more we begin to embody His characteristics. When a question is asked we know how He will answer because we know Him so well.

Consider your own relationships. Think about you and your spouse, parent or sibling, we know each other so well that we know how the other will answer. In those situations we can speak on behalf of those we have mentioned.

In these prayer situations we are speaking into situations and circumstances on behalf of our bridegroom Jesus. The more we know Him, the more intimate we are with Him, the more authority we carry.

In 2 Timothy 3:5 it is talking of the days I believe we can relate to. It reads

> *'holding to a form of godliness although they have denied its power; avoid such people as these.'* (NASB)

Holy Spirit quickened this to me dramatically. We have all heard and adopted psychological speak that is not Bible. The words He reminded me of were; "It takes seven positives to erase a negative!" We've heard it and probably repeated it. A great line to use to excuse a failure in prayer, how sad.

The other great sadness is; "If you are willing Lord". He most certainly is willing. That is why Jesus came to satisfy the debt, to redeem us, to buy us back. If you go and sell something to a pawnbroker and then go and pay the price necessary to reclaim ownership of the goods, you take the goods with you. That's what Jesus did, paid the price and we are His. Any further ministry that may be needed to cut off all the tentacles of the enemy is all on the basis that the price has already been paid! Jesus does not need to go back to the cross and neither do you.

This is what Holy Spirit said to me "DON'T YOU THINK I CAN DO IT THE FIRST TIME?" How easily we can deny the power. Let's repent as necessary and get back on track.

So by faith, start to visualise this and see that seed of faith flourishing. As you pray and ask "in the Name of Jesus", the hosts of heaven surround you and enforce that victory. All of a sudden "in the name of Jesus" moves from a heartfelt yet often pedestrian sign off to something completely powerful.

Our language must change instead of 'Lord I know that you can do such and such' to, 'Lord I know you will do it'. It is not presumption - I have the seed of faith, the word He quickened to me so I know He will. Thats Faith!

I was at a gathering of Apostles and Prophets on the Gold Coast, Australia in November 2019. During worship I felt someone touch my back. I turned to see who was there and there was no one near me. As I started to worship again, I again felt the touch on my back and a voice whispering in my ear so close I could feel the breath "I've got you, I've got your back!"

As events have unfolded into 2020 I saw that word, that seed of faith before me. I knew we were coming through, that we were thriving despite these circumstances.

We are indeed seated in heavenly places with Jesus, so we are definitely above the circumstances. Faith arises and strengthens as we meditate on the Word of God. We see with clarity that we are in the world but we are not of it. Putting our trust in Jesus the author and the finisher of our faith. Regardless of what is going on we are subject to heaven. We operate in the economy of heaven as we honour God with our tithing and sowing. He honours that faith.

This is not simply about the happenings of 2020. The truth is always the truth so we can apply it to any and every situation. The more we do that the more intimate we become with Jesus. The more we know who we are, not who we would like to be or hope to be. No.... who we already are, so when we call upon the name of Jesus it is powerful. We are calling upon His name in faith and that unleashes the power of heaven. Angels who have been waiting to hear the voice of His word and do it. (See Psalms 103:20)

Let's approach prayer according to the words of the Apostle John in 1 John 5:14-15.

'This is the confidence which we have before Him, that, if we ask anything according to His will, He hears us. And if we know that He hears us in whatever we ask, we know that we have the requests which we have asked from Him.' (NASB)

But how do I know His will? Know Him more!

CHAPTER 6

Fear Or Faith In The Face Of Fire

As we read Daniel 3, it was a time in history where to stand for what you believed ensured persecution. Let me elucidate, to stand in that day and say "I worship Jesus" would have left you open to persecution of the most horrific kind. Today where Christian nations and others who simply abhor the terrorist tactics of certain groups, those countries, cities have had the full force of hatred driven by satanic forces thrown at them.

What are we to do?

'Beloved, do not be surprised at the fiery ordeal among you, which comes upon you for your testing, as though something strange were happening

to you; but to the degree that you share the sufferings of Christ, keep on rejoicing, so that at the revelation of His glory you may rejoice and be overjoyed.' 1 Peter 4:12-13 (NASB)

The interesting thing about Shadrach, Meshach and Abed-nego was that they didn't have to go away and pray about it. They were ready as it says in 2 Timothy 4:2 '...be ready in season and out of season'. They were in unity! That is so powerful and God commanded the blessing as He said He would. (See Psalms 133)

'And they overcame him by the blood of the lamb and by the word of their testimony, and they did not love their lives to the death.' Revelation 12:11 (NKJV)

The extraordinary thing here is chronologically Jesus had not been born in the natural and most certainly had not been to the cross and so John had not been exiled to Patmos. Yet once again it seems the timeline folded and they were living out this scripture.

There are five key truths that we see in Daniel Chapter 3

1. You can expect to go through the fire. (Daniel 3:6, Luke 3:16, Malachi 3:2-3)

2. If we want to speak the Word of God we can expect to be refined. (Psalms 12:6)

3. You can trust God no matter what happens. (Daniel 3:16-17) Nebuchadnezzar came with the Godfather offer, "the offer they couldn't refuse". They left the consequences of their Godly choice to God. (Psalms 34:15-19, Proverbs 3:5,6, Psalms 37)

4. You can anticipate a change in your life. (Daniel 3:25)The fire will not effect you. (Daniel 3:27)

'Blessed is a man who perseveres under trial; for once he has been approved, he will receive the crown of life which the Lord has promised to those who love Him.' James 1:12 (NASB)

5. You can expect to experience prosperity. (Daniel 3:30) Not bowing down to the idols of the world.

'For I am confident of this very thing, that He who began a good work among you will complete it by the day of Christ Jesus.' Philippians 1:6 (NASB)

- Those who came through the fire were blessed by God.
- God is not just interested in doing for you but rather in you.
- You will find God is always with you in the fire

(Daniel 3:25).

'For it is He who rescues you from the net of the trapper And from the deadly plague. He will cover you with His pinions, And under His wings you may take refuge; His faithfulness is a shield and wall. You will not be afraid of the terror by night, Or of the arrow that flies by day; Of the plague that stalks in darkness, Or of the destruction that devastates at noon. A thousand may fall at your side And ten thousand at your right hand, But it shall not approach you. You will only look on with your eyes And see the retaliation against the wicked. For you have made the LORD, my refuge, The Most High, your dwelling place.' Psalms 91:3-9 (NASB)

'When you pass through the waters, I will be with you; And through the rivers, they will not overflow you. When you walk through the fire, you will not be scorched, Nor will the flame burn you.' Isaiah 43:2 (NASB)

Who is this fourth man? Was It Jesus? Was it Holy Spirit? Was it an angel? I guess the only comment to be made is the fourth man was entirely supernatural and sent from the spirit realm to answer Shadrach, Meshach and Abed-nego's prayer. Remember what they said to Nebuchadnezzar in verse 17

'If it be so, our God whom we serve is able to rescue us from the furnace of blazing fire; and He will rescue us from your hand, O king. But even if He does not, let it be known to you, O king, that we are not going to serve your gods nor worship the golden statue that you have set up.'
Daniel 3:17-18 *(NASB)*

Note the three things in their statement:

1. Our God is able.

2. Our God is willing however even if He does not we won't bow down to you or your gods. (Shadrach, Meshach and Abed-nego did not have the access to heaven that we have and yet they had a relationship with the Father that we should all desire.)

3. They did not love their lives unto death.

If God's purposes were better served by not delivering them they were okay with that. They reverenced God in a way we seldom see today but when we do it is truly inspirational. When we understand His ways are not our ways they are so much higher, He accomplishes so much more in one act and sometimes we can forget that.

This is why that seed of faith is so important, we start to see the end from the beginning. We are going through!

So what is that idol that the king of this world is asking you to bow down to?

There are so many pressures in life pushing in on us until we don't feel like we can stand against them but we don't go by feelings. Fear is overwhelming in our society today and we have the answer - Faith in Christ Jesus. Faith displaces fear and as we allow our faith seeds to germinate and flourish they kick fear out forever.

I am not moved by circumstances.

I am not moved by feelings.

I am moved by the Word of God.

'Woe to those who call evil good, and good evil; Who substitute darkness for light and light for darkness; Who substitute bitter for sweet and sweet for bitter!' Isaiah 5:20 (NASB)

CHAPTER 7

Which Faith?

I was thinking about faith and it occurred to me that not all faith is the same. In fact not all faith is faith!

So many things creep into our language that actually dilute the power of the words spoken. We actually need to retrain, renew our minds daily.

> 'And do not be conformed to this world, but be transformed by the renewing of your mind, so that you may prove what the will of God is, that which is good and acceptable and perfect.'
> Romans 12:2 (NASB)

How do we fulfil our need for new input? We must read the Word and let it seep into us. Read it with fresh eyes, always asking Holy Spirit to reveal Truth to us. Then we need to meditate on the words, the revelations that we receive until they become a living reality.

We can all believe something in an intellectual way and not accept it as a truth by which we can live our lives. We have to graduate beyond belief to faith. There is a difference between the two. It is now no longer the time to simply give intellectual ascent to the Bible, but rather embrace it as the reality by which we can live our lives.

We talk about alignment often, being aligned with apostolic leaders in our stream, or of the same tribe. Let me say that is great as far as it goes and we should find where we fit. The much bigger question is our belief system aligned with God's truth? Are our hearts aligned with His?

These are not simply throw away lines, they are matters to be pondered. We must be really honest with ourselves and God. If we feel there may be a deviation, schism or differing of opinion with God, allow the Lord to speak into that and bring us into all truth.

Remembering always if there is a fault it's not in God. That is truly what alignment is all about - recognising there has been a straying off the narrowpath, then allowing Holy Spirit to gently and lovingly guide us to the correct path.

This could be termed a mid course correction. It's not anymore than repenting and returning. When we pray in faith we know that we are going through whatever it is.

So that's one part of this and then there's the fear that masquerades as faith. Prayers that are not motivated by faith in God, instead driven by fear that something bad is happening or about to happen. When prayer is offered this way the premise is that hopefully they will prevent said catastrophe. Unfortunately because they are motivated by fear and not faith they have no power. Even as the words are spoken the seed of faith is being stomped on.

As Christians, believers in the truth of God's Word, we must be totally sold out to that. Not be like those who pray and often because of disappointment know as they do, they have no vision for healing, deliverance or miracles. So whilst the words may be said the heart conviction is not there.

Faith is more than blab it and grab it!

Faith is a heart condition.

'For as he thinks in his heart, so is he…..' Proverbs 23:7a (NKJV)

'Watch over your heart with all diligence, for from it flow the springs of life.' Proverbs 4:23 (NASB)

Something we are not conditioned to note is Truth and Fact are not synonymous. They are quite different - Truth is eternal - Fact is temporal. We see this all the time in the scientific community. As there are new discoveries, facts change.

As we agree with God and stand firmly on His truth we graduate to a different kind of faith. The faith that hears the Word and yields to it.

The Bible is full of countless examples of this kind of faith.

- Abraham and Sarah standing firm for their own child, although physically it was impossible.
- Abraham knowing God would provide the sacrifice on Mount Moriah.
- The Shunammite woman who Elisha prophesied would have a son.
- Esther and Mordecai with King Ahasuerus.
- Ruth and Naomi with Boaz.
- Rahab and the fall of Jericho.
- David as he conquered Goliath.
- Elijah vanquishing the 400 prophets of Baal.

I love the story of Isaac in Genesis 26 where he sowed seed in a land of drought and famine. He was sowing seeds of faith and he reaped a great harvest. The Bible records that he reaped a hundredfold harvest in that year and God blessed him. He became rich and grew richer until he became very wealthy. There is a supernatural wisdom to sowing seeds of faith in order that any harvest blessings which are received are then administered with great wisdom. Just as Joseph administered Egypt's food wealth in the seven year famine. Joseph trusted, had faith in God's strategy for the situation and that's exactly what we need today.

They had a faith that went so far beyond praying for a carpark. These people are just a handful, please read your Bible and find your own faith heroes and be inspired by them.

I sometimes think because of the times and the comfort we live in we don't need that desperate kind of faith. To that I would say is there any other kind?

CHAPTER 8

The Gift Of Faith

1 Corinthians 12 introduces the nine gifts of the Holy Spirit from verse 8. They are outlined as follows:

- The Word of Wisdom
- The Word of (revelation) Knowledge
- The Gift of Faith
- Gifts of Healings
- Working of Miracles
- The Gift of Prophecy
- Discerning of Spirits
- The Gift of Speaking in various Tongues
- Interpretation of Tongues

Those who move in the Gift of Faith believe God in such a way, that He honours their word as His own and miraculously brings it to pass.

The Gift of Faith is a power gift the same as miracles and healings and as such they will often be in operation together. The Gift of Faith as with the other 8 gifts is given by Holy Spirit, there is an interesting line in verse 7, it reads

> *"But to each one is given the manifestation of the Spirit for the common good."* 1 Corinthians 12:7
> (NASB)

The thing about the Gift of Faith and in fact each gift of the Holy Spirit is that they are gifts. And when you consider a gift it has to be received, opened and then utilised. Any gift can only be utilised as we have an understanding of its use. The Gift of Faith is a powerful and quite frankly awesome gift from the throne of God.

The Gift of Faith is not simply regular faith. Also it is not regular faith just amped up a little, it's a whole different level of faith altogether. When we consider healing, we know scripture tells us that each one can lay hands upon the sick and they will recover. The Gift of Healings however is quite different in power and operation. The same is true for the Gift of Faith.

The Word of Knowledge is a message straight from

the Father giving us an insight into what is happening, something that is unseen or unknown to us in the natural. The Word of Knowledge used in concert with other gifts of the Holy Spirit, I believe was what Jesus was talking about when He said He only did what He saw His Father doing.

For each one of us we need to learn from Holy Spirit how to use these gifts for the purpose that they are given. Perhaps a good analogy is that you would not give your car keys to a child that had not learned and mastered the mechanics of driving and the rules of the road. A car can be powerful and used incorrectly, a deadly weapon. My prayer is that we would understand the Gift of Faith and use it as the Father purposes.

The Passion Translation says,

'Each believer is given continuous revelation by the Holy Spirit to benefit not just himself but all.'
1 Corinthians 12:7 (TPT)

These gifts are given to be given and to be used freely as you minister. An interesting point to note is that Holy Spirit will distribute or release the gifts according to what you have need of at a particular time.

Let's think about Moses now - okay I know he had not had the pentecost experience but he met with God in a way few ever do. When the Egyptians were chasing the Hebrews to the edge of the Red Sea, Moses needed help from heaven, he needed a miracle. The Lord gave him the strategy to tell the people to go forward, lift his staff and stretch his hand over the water to part the waters. Now that was the miracle, the sea parted then the Gift of Faith was needed to keep it parted.

This Gift of Faith is not the faith spoken of as 'fruit of the spirit' in Galatians 5:22-23 (which incidentally is faithfulness which is quite different to Faith).

'But the fruit of the Spirit is love, joy, peace, patience, kindness, goodness, faithfulness, gentleness, self-control; against such things there is no law.' Galations 5:22-23 (NASB)

It is not like the general faith we have spoken of previously and by which we ordinarily receive answers to our prayers. It is not the saving faith by which we all received salvation, it is different. It is special, given by God in circumstances where it is necessary. It is important to note there are different types of faith just as there are different types of prayer and it is our loss if we just call them all the same.

The Gift of Faith is a supernatural endowment given by the Holy Spirit. As a result of the gift, that which is spoken by God or man will come to pass. Whether it is a prophetic utterance, miracle assurance, blessing or curse, creation or destruction, or alteration, it will ultimately come to pass when spoken by this gift. As you can see the power of death and life is in the power of the tongue, this gift must be exercised in great wisdom and humility. The Gift of Faith has the ability to see through mountains, to see around corners, to see further because it is literally God's sight. And that therefore is the caution that it must be exercised as I said with great wisdom and humility.

The Gift of Miracles would perform a miracle, the Gift of Faith would receive it. It expects the miracle!

The Gift of Faith was in operation with the patriarchs for supernatural blessing. Abraham, Isaac and Joseph commanded blessings, often times they did not see it for years but they believed and expected it and it manifested.

The Gift of Faith was in operation for Daniel's protection in the Lions den in Daniel 6.

It provided supernatural sustenance for Elijah by the Brook Cherith. The Gift of Faith is at work with other gifts in the raising of the dead, in deliverance from evil spirits. It is also noted in Galatians 3:5

> *'So then, does He who provides you with the Spirit and works miracles among you, do it by works of the Law, or by hearing with faith?'* (NASB)

Gift of Faith and David

When David went down to meet Goliath he was not operating presumption.

He prophesied in 1 Samuel 17:46

'This day the Lord will hand you over to me, and I will strike you and remove your head from you. Then I will give the dead bodies of the army of the Philistines this day to the birds of the sky and the wild animals of the earth, so that all the earth may know that there is a God in Israel.' (NASB)

He had the prophetic word and the Gift of Faith backed it. Sometimes the prophetic needs the Gift of Faith. Not that the Word of God won't work, it is more to protect the word until it manifests.

Sometimes I see it as though it is a God bubble that I am inside of with divine protection all around me. The bubble is transparent so I can still see the negatives outside yet they cannot touch me or the manifestation of God's promise in the situation.

CHAPTER 9

Faith And The Seer

I was considering that the Lord is releasing the seer gifting prolifically across the body of believers right now. I know God doesn't do anything randomly or without a strategy.

Most people we meet have a measure of the seer and I would like to propose that this increase is related to Faith. The gift is not simply about visions or dreams, it is about the understanding and interpreting of those things.

At this time I believe God is using the seer gifting to release faith. It is so much more than just giving a word or an interpretation. It is about stewarding what God has given watching over the word, protecting it, watering it and seeing it come to fruition.

When I was very young I was told, "When you get

a word just put it away and forget about it, you can't make it happen", which is of course true however, my Bible says we are co-labourers with Christ so perhaps we are meant to be involved. The punchline was, "If God wants that for you He'll make it happen, so just forget it".

As I've grown, I believe prophetic words, dreams and visions are gifts from the throne. Of course you need to discern the spirits - so be careful who speaks over you. Stay well connected with Godly people, leaders and those who are further down the road than you, they will protect you. And of course none of those are a substitute for your own intimate relationship with The Lord.

The most important thing in our lives is relationship with The Father through Jesus Christ. Look for those people that Holy Spirit brings across your path in whom you recognise Godly character.

Psalms 37 would cause me to believe God would not give a dream or vision or promise if He did not intend for it to manifest, He does not tempt or frustrate us.

Psalms 8:5-6 says to me that God is invested in our success and in our victories. So if He has whispered it to us in a dream or a vision or a prophetic word, He's invested in seeing that come to pass. We just have to agree in faith.

We must always base our beliefs on the infallible Word of God. In relation to the subject of seers, who do I instantly think of? Isaiah, Ezekiel and the Apostle John. I am not saying they are the only ones, they are just some of the ones who saw in the spirit realm very clearly things beyond their understanding. They did not allow those visions to fall to the ground and die. They watched over them, they recorded them, and because of their stewardship and wisdom we are today receiving more revelation of those visions and dreams, as we see them manifest.

Then of course when we consider Joseph and Daniel who both had an incredible ability to interpret dreams which changed the course of history. They also operated in the Word of Knowledge - a knowing of what dreams had been dreamt without the dreamer recounting it.

I therefore believe that seers must watch over the vision, word, the seed, the dream. If we've seen it in the spirit realm (whilst that is awesome) it is not much use to us unless we see it manifest here. And like wise if you receive a word, a dream, a promise and you know it is a word from God, you can draw it into your reality as you fix your eyes of faith on it. Start to put flesh on it.

Just a cautionary note: Please don't do this with people unless you have their permission to agree with them as it can be interpreted as manipulation or spiritual witchcraft. You can pray protection particularly for family members however, please steer clear of calling people into or out of relationships no matter how well-meaning you believe your motives are. God in His great wisdom gave each one of us a free will. He will allow us to make our own choices and go our own way, and so should we!

The only thing we can and in fact must do is by our own lives show there is a better way. There are always blessings as we choose the right way. Even as we make those God choices we must believe in faith and not adopt an attitude toward God of "well I did that so you must do this".

It delights God's heart as He sees His design coming together. The many and varied gifts dovetailing together as we see, none of them should operate in isolation - we are so much better, stronger together.

Faith does not twist God's arm, faith simply trusts.

CHAPTER 10

Promises Received

"God is not a man, that He would lie, Nor a son of man, that He would change His mind; Has He said, and will He not do it? Or has He spoken, and will He not make it good?" Numbers 23:19 (NASB)

I love that passage of scripture, God doesn't lie and He doesn't change His mind on promises made.

The only problem is that we don't always believe that. Our faith is fractured, damaged in someway, often times the damage is done through our experience.

Our experiences which we are not denying still come under the Lordship of Jesus Christ and are therefore not penultimate. We must place our history at the foot of the cross. Yield our past to Jesus.

'*... and whatever is not from faith is sin"* Romans 14:23b (NASB)

Now I know Paul was originally talking about food but I do not believe the truth of that word is limited to food.

We need to rethink our believing, that is what we are talking about in regard to this new operating system. We cannot simply overlay the new so that when the new is not to our liking we revert to the old, the comfortable. Old is what seems to be comfortable because it is familiar but may not be comfortable in the long term. The Lord desires that we move up from glory to glory as 2 Corinthians 3:18 puts it,

> *'But we all, with unveiled faces, looking as in a mirror at the glory of the Lord, are being transformed into the same image from glory to glory, just as from the Lord, the Spirit.'* (NASB)

Just as scientists tell us the Universe which God is still creating is ever expanding, we are to keep growing in faith, wisdom, understanding, knowledge and so on. Never stand still - there is always more.

So back to the promises which we must receive by faith. Mark 11:22-24 is one of the great promises. Look at verse 23:

'Truly I say to you, whoever says to this

mountain, 'Be taken up and thrown into the sea,' **AND DOES NOT DOUBT IN HIS HEART**, *but believes that what he says is going to happen,* **IT WILL BE GRANTED TO HIM."** (The emphasis is mine because I want for you to see the connection.)

We doubt for many reasons. Perhaps we have prayed and earnestly believed before and it did not happen, so will it happen this time?

We may doubt because we've never seen what we're believing for happen.

We are not doubting the words we speak or the prayers we pray, realistically we are doubting God.

I can hear the outrage …. "It's His word. He said it."

As long as we are praying in line with His word it must happen. Isaiah 55:11 tells us that is so, His word never returns to Him void/empty. It always accomplishes what He desires, it always succeeds in the matter for which He sent it.

We must be like Jesus. He said He only did what He saw the Father doing. So our intimate relationship with God is key in this particular area of mountain moving faith. We need to get God's wisdom and then speak.

A cautionary note: Gods answer is not always going to be manifested in the way we expect, so it is most important to remember God is working everything together for good. As we walk through these times with the Lord our faith grows as our love for Him and trust in Him deepens.

So how do we combat doubt? There are many things I can suggest that I practice in my own life.

- Worship (not simply singing but a lifestyle)

'When you live a life of abandoned love, surrendered before the awe of God, here's what you'll experience: Abundant life. Continual protection. And complete satisfaction!' Proverbs 19:23 (TPT)

- Meditate on a Word - Just be with God and let Him infuse His truth and possibilities in you.

- Refuse negativity - Guard yourself against those who may criticise your stand.

- Guard your tongue - Be the Shunammite in 2 Kings 4:8-37. When people asked her what was going on her response was 'It will be well' and 'It is well'. She was agreeing with God and she received her son back.

I am aware some people would call her posture hyper-faith. I am not clear on that. I know that woman would have had all sorts of emotions surging through her however, she held fast to her faith - now that's hyper-faith! News flash it's right there in the Bible, I did not make it up. Perhaps, just perhaps that is what is needed in this New Era with this new operating system.

As you read your Bible there are so many promises and no one has a monopoly on any one promise, they are available to all who believe and do not doubt.

CHAPTER 11

It Is Finished

When Jesus hung on the cross and as He gave up His spirit, He cried out 'It is finished'. The question then is of course asked, what is finished? Over the years there have been many answers to that question, all of which seemed to touch the truth yet not answer the enquiry.

I was discussing this with a friend Adrian Beale and he proposed the answer is of course everything, it is all finished! I started to ponder on that as I did not want another partial answer. The fullness can only come by revelation to your spirit.

How's this?

Every aspect of the atonement is fully satisfied, the debt has been paid in full and there is nothing more for us to do.

Now most Christians will be saying 'I know that I went to bible college,' (so did I). So what is the fullness of this? What is the thing that we haven't fully grasped and therefore have not fully experienced? Now here's the thing - the first intention of God was to have family, have relationship, Him with us and us with Him. Adam the first man sinned and was banished from the garden. He effectively lost everything God provided in the garden.

What did he lose? Protection, fellowship/connection with God, health, prosperity, innocence and because of the curse he lost his God given ability to subdue and have dominion over demonic entities. In other words he was fair game for the enemy. Now in our natural selves we may be able to subdue and so on but without Christ the target is usually other people, either individuals or entire cultural or religious groups. That was never what God intended and that is the perversion of the enemy.

When Jesus said "It is finished!" And then down through time millions of believers said Amen - So be it, by receiving Jesus Christ as their Lord and Saviour. I believe He was opening the gate to the garden. The angels guarding it stand aside to allow believers free access to everything the garden provides. It is finished is total restoration of everything that was lost at the fall of man.

What moves God? I believe the answer is faith.

Now we know that 1 Corinthians 13:13 tells us Faith, Hope and Love abide and the greatest of these is love. What it doesn't say is the other two are unimportant. We know love, the agape God kind of love can transform everything you just need the faith to believe it will.

> *'But if any of you lacks wisdom, let him ask of God, who gives to all generously and without reproach, and it will be given to him. But he must ask in faith without any doubting, for the one who doubts is like the surf of the sea, driven and tossed by the wind. For that person ought not to expect that he will receive anything from the Lord,' James 1:5-7* (NASB)

Nothing wavering, we must be steadfast regardless of what we may see or hear. We have been given authority over all those things, it is probably overdue that we start to behave like the conquerers, the overcomers we were destined to be. Then, and only then will we consistently see harvest time!

We live in a cynical society. Doubt and disbelief are rampaging through every area of life. Doubt and disbelief cannot co-exist with faith, it is an either or situation. Doubt will delay your harvest or destroy it. So we must have that spark of hope so faith can become the substance of that hope. Faith destroys doubt!

Faith honours God so I must boldly say, doubt and disbelief dishonour God. This is not a minor misstep this is serious. The exciting thing is as we honour God with our faith, God honours faith. Our harvest is assured.

So why is it so many good, nice Christians live in continual disappointment and defeat?

Then there are others who appear to succeed at everything. It is as though they live in a different realm, a realm of continuing favour. Everything about them thrives and flourishes as the word says in Deuteronomy 28:7b everything you put your hand to shall prosper (paraphrased). They are evidently blessed in relationships, career, health and material possessions, they all seem to be vibrant with goodness and fruitfulness.

The third group live in kind of a no mans land. Sometimes things work out and blessing flows and other times nothing seems to come together and the blessing is not present. Their lives are a combination of blessing and curse and not much to celebrate. Unfortunately this is not only normal for many people - most believe this is normal.

I am not saying there won't be battles, obstacles, mountains - call them what you will. What I am saying is you can expect victory!

I have always struggled with ministries being labelled as Hyper-Faith. I am not sure what that means, and I am not their judge. On that subject, personally I believe "Hyper-Faith" is not generally that which we would term Faith anyway. It may be "I am going to win millions of dollars in the lottery and when I get that I will tithe or sow". WRONG - sow from what is in your hand and God will bring the increase. That is the truth of the word so grow your faith around that. These maybe wishful thoughts, which as appealing as they seem in the moment they are not faith.

Another perhaps more concerning point that does effect each one of us, as it reflects badly upon the body, is the belief that God is going to answer from heaven and I don't need to do anything - it's all about Him. That is the cleverness of this deception because of course we know it's all about Him. However, we must never forget if we're not experiencing the fulness that was promised right now WE need to make some changes. Then all of heaven will move!

What changes you ask? Well, that is between you and Holy Spirit. He will convict you as to whatever needs attention. If it's not of God it's sin - there is no middle ground. There is always the argument made that it may be man, (a third option) ourselves, our fleshy nature. That is possibly true however, if we, no matter how spiritual we think we are do not agree with the One True Living God then we're wrong and that's sin.

In the western world we find the word 'sin' offensive (which it should be) but not for the reasons you would think. First world people seem to like a softer approach, it maybe 'error'. Just "oops I missed it". I am sorry, if we are not in sync with God we are in sin.

Let Holy Spirit show you and then quickly repent - there is no judgement in repentance, just get back on the right track. Prepare to receive your harvest.

I believe the Bible is God's love letter to us. It is full of everything we need to be in health and prosper. We only need to take the words of power and plant them in our lives as God purposed for us to do.

When Holy Spirit breathed inspiration into the authors of the individual scrolls, He was breathing truth - the eternal truth of heaven for us to live our lives by.

Of course revelation, fresh manna is still being released by the Spirit every day. It will not ever disprove, criticise or make moot the canon of scripture. That would be another spirit.

You reap what you sow. A well tended garden will bring a bountiful harvest.

So there are several points to consider.

Seed, watering, fertilizer/feeding the growing plants, sunlight, protection from wind, initial soil preparation. No this is not a gardening book. Remember where God started in Genesis 1 in the garden.

Psalms 103:1-5 talks of Him pardoning all our iniquities and healing all our diseases. All means all. There is nothing too difficult for God.

There are always reasons why the 'all' may not be happening in your life. I encourage you to take that up with the Lord. He will uncover the blockages and if you let Him, He will work with you to achieve breakthrough.

Always remember this, success and prosperity are relative. Our walk with the Lord is never a competition. We must not covet someone else's blessing, that will kill our harvest.

A couple of interesting thoughts around seeds and harvest. We all know there are many, many varieties of plants, trees and shrubs. We tend to look at what is above the ground and that confirms to us things are going well, all true. However what is happening below ground level is actually what influences the harvest. Are the roots strong? Are they well fed and watered? Do they have enough room to spread and grow? These are extremely important points that require our attention as they relate to our lives.

Some plants are annuals, some are bi-annuals and some are perennials. Which harvest are we looking for, a one off? Or perhaps a couple of returns or are we prepared to plant the correct seed and care for it to have an ongoing harvest?

Let me finish with this, you deserve a good harvest. It is the result of a Spiritual Law, we always reap as we sow. From this day forward let us determine to sow good faith seed, then care for that seed of faith, so a good harvest is inevitable.

CHAPTER 12

Jack

In the midst of writing this on the evening of June 11th 2021, we lost a beloved member of our family. Our darling Jack, he is a Samriever (Samoyed x Golden Retriever) and when he left us he was 13 1/2 in human years.

I say this because I believe he is with the Lord in heaven so he 'is' not was. Now I am not trying to mess-up your theology, I am just trying to communicate my belief through our experience. He was a gift to us from the Lord and not just a pet but a true member of the family and therefore our faith is the Lord is caring for him because He cares for us. It takes no more faith to believe he is with the Lord than to believe our cherished family and friends are there waiting for us. It is simply the box we have put God in. We have limited the limitless power of the God who created all things. He is love and the gifts He gives us to love and be loved by on this earth I believe are waiting for us.

Your image of heaven maybe different to mine and that's okay. Love, joy, peace, patience, kindness, goodness, faithfulness, gentleness, self control are the attributes of the Holy Spirit, the fruit of the Spirit if you like and heaven will reflect those in every facet of its existence. So, as long as our vision of heaven encapsulates those realities the particulars maybe as different as you and I.

My Bible tells me the Holy Spirit is our comforter so I know He wanted to comfort us in our heartbreak. In whatever ways were personal to us, to bind up our broken hearts with His great love for us.

While he was on this earth, every prayer meeting, Bible study, board meeting and BBQ Jack was front and usually in the centre. He responded to praying in tongues and worship because he was surrounded by it. He was always around as I decreed the Word over situations.

He and his sister Mya saw angels, let me explain. In our home we had a very wide hallway leading from the front to the living kitchen area in the centre of the home. On one particular day Jack was in the front bedroom which he often was so he could see what was going on in the park across the street. We called him and he came to the door of that room and he wouldn't move into the hallway, let me hasten to add he wasn't frightened or barking just transfixed. We tried to encourage him to come but no. I jotted off a quick memo to the Lord why wouldn't he move, show us what was going on. Instantly I saw a huge angel filling the hallway. The angel moved a little to one side and then Jack walked past.

That is only one time, trust me there were many. Over the course of his time on earth there were so many examples of similar encounters. Why because we are special? Well of course the answer is yes! We are however, so are you - it was simply a matter of our loving Father opening our minds to embrace a part of Him that was always available to us. We were operating in an old system that may have talked of the possibilities of God but never really expected or explored them.

In the depth of our sorrow I cried out to God that Hebrews 11:1 promises that 'faith is the assurance or substance of things hoped for the evidence of things not yet seen'. I told the Lord that I needed the assurance, the substance of my faith. That was in the middle of the night.

The next day my sister who lives in another state called me and related a dream she had where she was on the beach with her dog and Jack and he was fit, well, young and enjoying life. That made me cry - I missed him so desperately.

Then our son who lives in the United States called me and related a dream he had. Jack was in a large green space, a meadow or very large lawn and he was running and interacting with the people around him, that seemed familiar with and they knew him. He was fit and well and young and Todd's words 'he is living his best life'. What we have here is a shadow of what is to come.

My point with these stories is God answered my prayer before I prayed it. That night I also had a dream and I very seldom dream and it woke me it was so real. I was in the garden with Jack and he came bouncing towards me with his tail wagging furiously and as he wagged his tail his whole body wagged, he was fit and well and young again.

My very dear friend Cheryl Lindley pointed out to me the dreams were different yet all confirmation of the same thing. Three confirmations. Yes and Amen!

We know so little of God compared to what there is to know. That is what this Now Word of Faith is about. Embracing this new operating system in every area of life, allowing Holy Spirit to permeate every fibre of our lives and breathe new life into us.

For me I know God gave me Jack to teach me to love unconditionally, I am still not perfect at it but praise God because of Jack I am aware and growing in that. Now you may disagree but that is my experience not my opinion. In this time instead of disagreeing with someones experience how about we ask the Lord to make it real to us.

John G Lake said 'Friends, when a Christian tries to live by reason, he is moving out of God's country into the enemy's land. We belong in the miraculous or supernatural realm. Christ was a miracle. Every Christian is a miracle. Every answer to prayer is a miracle. Every divine illumination is a miracle.'

The very fact that we are in this world is testimony to the miraculous so let's not just pay it lip service but truly embrace the miracle realisation of our high calling.

By Faith our responsibility is to say to those mountains, "Move" and do not doubt but believe and we will see things we never expected to.

According to your faith, be it so unto you….and according to my faith be it so unto me.

In my dark hours of grief and sorrow the word came to me, "I work all things together for good for those who love and are called to my purposes".

Let me tell you, I wasn't thrilled or comforted by those words at that moment however, over the following days God has done remarkable miraculous works in me and the family.

For myself, strange as it may seem I believe He has lifted me to a higher level of anointing and authority, now my responsibility is to walk in that. As for the rest of the family theirs is not my story to tell, suffice to say everyone has had a very special touch of heaven which changes everything.

CHAPTER 13

Faith In Action

'But do you want to know, O foolish man, that faith without works is dead?' James 2:20 (NKJV)

I am sure your have heard many sermons based around this scripture, I know I have. As a young person hearing the range of beliefs that emanated from this were indeed very confusing! My starting place back then which has seen me in good stead for life was God is not a God of confusion. So I began the onerous task of unravelling what God had in fact said, what had been taught and how personal experiences had influenced our version of this truth.

Experience is a big one obviously as we're talking about peoples lives. I want to stress none of this is to criticise or even correct. It is only to inspire. To see that no matter how big our image of God is - He is bigger. No matter where our faith level is - there is another level where we can indeed experience the supernatural as our way of life. So in response I would say what the scripture says,

> '...."It shall be done to you according to your faith."' *Matthew 9:29* (NASB1995)

There is another scripture which does not mention faith and yet I believe it is the embodiment of abandoned faith in Luke 1:38

> 'And Mary said, "Behold, the Lord's bond-servant; may it be done to me according to your word." And the angel departed from her.' (NASB)

How many of us actually take God at His word? So my take on James 2:20 is when we get a word, a vision or a dream first of all hide it in your heart, meditate on it so faith does grow and then follow the path He leads us on. Go through the doors that may have previously been shut. Cast aside the failures and disappointments of the past in the assurance that He is doing a new thing in us and with us.

Most importantly rest in what He has promised. He, more than anyone knows exactly where your faith level is currently. That is what He said to the blind men, 'According to their faith' not yours and not mine. There are times as we have mentioned when the Gift of Faith is in operation and has the supernatural ability to carry others with it, parting of the Red Sea and so on.

The greatest encouragement I can give is Faith grows, increases, strengthens as you use it. If you don't use it you run the risk of having your faith atrophy just as any muscle that is not used. It will weaken over time.

When God gives me a word, dream or vision, I always seek for a strategy to fulfil the promise. Don't run ahead of God - let's be more like Jesus and only do what we see the Father doing.

At this point, I believe it is important to remember everything in God works together for good. All the giftings, callings, ministries - all the functions of the Body of Christ work together and should work together, otherwise we are not cohesive. We are simply individuals fulfilling our own needs, wants and/or desires. That, my friends is not one body. It is simply a lot of individual cells perhaps randomly colliding from time to time, not always with the best results.

Let me propose that Faith is the glue that holds all this together.

I wanted to include some real life testimonies where the fruit from a seed of faith manifested. These are not included as doctrine, as God may not do something the same way twice but rather as inspiration to embark you on your own adventure in faith.

Testimony 1

I remember in the middle of a particularly cold winter I received a call from my friend. She began to tell me about a lady in the church her parents went to who had an inoperable brain tumour. All the pastors in the church had prayed for her, every visiting Ministry they could think of had prayed for her. Then someone had suggested perhaps they call me. The pastoral oversight of their church had no objection since she had only been given hours to live. That was a Friday afternoon. As I drove that 30 minutes to the hospice I felt quite inadequate. I was desperately seeking the Lord for an awesome prayer so I looked the part. However, the only word the Lord gave me was "Blessed is he who comes in the name of the Lord".

So I entered her room on that word. What I observed was frankly quite daunting so I shut my eyes, I wanted to see heaven and only heaven. So with the word the Lord had given me in my ears I approached her bed. She was blown up with fluid retention and her major organs were all ceasing to work. In fact, the catheter that had been inserted to drain fluid was no longer functioning.

What I learned that night was in my inadequacy God is more than able. As I decreed healing over her body, the catheter was literally washed out of her as a rush of fluid was released from her body. Before our eyes the swelling from the fluid in her body disappeared.

At that point there was an invasion of medical staff as they were convinced something had gone terribly wrong. I waited in the hall for a couple of minutes and then her son came out telling me his mother wanted to see me.

She was sitting up in the bed fully conscious with a healthy colour restored to her skin. She called me by name and I looked around at her family because she didn't know me. No one in the room had told her my name. She relayed to me that an angel had told her my name.

The doctor and nurses had no idea what had happened, I just said God turned up. I said goodbye and left her with her family.

I was pleased to hear that two days later they released her and at that point I lost contact with her but I believe she lived for quite some time afterwards.

Testimony 2

A very close friend of my Mum and Dad's was in the intensive care unit of the local hospital. He had been diagnosed with some sort of cyst on his brain.

He was unconscious in that he had no idea what was going on around about him. He had an extremely high temperature and was obviously distressed. My Mum wanted to go and pray for him so I drove her. When we got to the ICU ordinarily they would've only let one of us in, however on this occasion we were both allowed to go in.

The sight that greeted us was definitely as distressing as we'd been told. At the same time I could 'see him whole', standing up straight and without pain. With the staff all hovering we decided to just pray in tongues because they might think we're foreign. I stayed at the foot of the bed with Mum at the head of the bed and we prayed in tongues, laid hands on him and decreed healing. After about five minutes we both felt it was done. He was peaceful and for now that was enough - for us anyway.

As we left the room his wife was outside so it was perfect timing for her to go in and sit with him.

About 3 o'clock in the afternoon his wife rang to tell my Mum he was awake and asking for us. Later that afternoon we returned to the hospital to see a totally different man, he was awake and alert. The tests they had conducted confirmed that the cyst was gone, his bloods were normal, his temperature and blood pressure were all normal.

The interesting thing was that even in that unconscious state he had known we were there. He also knew that we were decreeing healing over him in a language he didn't know and yet he understood.

He went home to live a long healthy life and on the strength of what had just happened, accepted Jesus Christ as his Lord.

Testimony 3

My husband Paul and I were invited to go to The Democratic Republic of Congo (DRC) and we both had a very strong 'yes' from God.

He told me we would carry words of life to that nation. On one particular day we were visiting a hospital which our partner ran. This was very exciting for me as I am passionate about releasing the healing power of God wherever I go.

The language barrier was quite significant but I was carrying a word of life and somehow I knew the Lord would make a way. We started in one ward and as our friend encouraged us to greet the people I knew I had a mandate from God to lay hands on the sick and see them recover. So I just began going from bed to bed praying in tongues over each one.

There were people of all ages with all sorts of ailments from Malaria to Typhoid, from HIV to malnutrition. So by faith I was laying hands on them and decreeing the word of life.

In the last ward there was a lady who couldn't even lift her head off the pillow. As I approached I saw that she was very bloated was clearly in a great deal of pain.

She understood no English and very little French as she spoke a dialect that was very hard for me to make sense of but I knew she was in desperate need of the healing touch of God.

I laid my hands on her decreeing in English and in tongues the finished work of the cross.

As I turned to leave the room one of the nurses came back and she asked if I had prayed for that lady, I said "Yes" of course. She told me there was no hope of life for her as she had stage 4 Pancreatic cancer. I just said "It is well".

We went down to the administration office to find Paul then there was an explosion of African jubilation. As I turned to see what was happening I saw the woman who could not lift her head from the pillow up dancing with about half a dozen others.

Wow!

The footnote to that is she actually was Rwandan and had trekked across the mountains to get to the hospital and a couple of days later she walked home back over the mountains.

Before we left DRC we founded a prayer ministry to be based at the hospital to pray for the sick. They started with 3 people coming together on a Saturday to pray for the sick within a month they had over 50 coming to pray and many miraculous testimonies. At that point I suggested they would go out into the town to pray for the sick and preach the good news .

The whole town was miraculously transformed.

We have many more testimonies of miracles and healings as we stepped out on the Word of Faith.

We've left some pages blank at the end for you to add some of your own.

It is important to remember the victories. As David went to face Goliath he reminded himself he had killed the lion, he had killed the bear so who is this uncircumcised Philistine that would stand before the armies of the Living God.

When we go to face our Goliaths we are never alone.

The Hosts of heaven are with us.

CHAPTER 14

What To Do When Faith Seems Weak?

Inevitably we will come to a time when we really have to push through. That would be the time when your faith really kicks in.

As new Christians, building our faith and getting to know Jesus and God the Father in a more intimate way, we find that things seem to happen much quicker. However as we grow in faith and relationship we discover that perhaps the Godhead isn't the ATM we had presumed they were. What do I mean by that? Well consider we need some cash so we go to the ATM, put our card in and provided we have cash in our account we can get cash out. It's a painless and reasonably instant transaction. Unfortunately for the modern day Christian we have demeaned God to that place of instant transaction.

Now whilst we all love an instant answer, experience has taught me that we learn precious little from that experience.

So the inevitability is that instant isn't always going to be the response. Please understand I'm not saying that God can't or won't answer us instantly. What I am saying is He loves us so much that through every circumstance His desire is for us to grow. He desires for us to know Him not just by what He does but by who He is. The children of Israel knew His deeds or works. Moses knew His thoughts. Moses had an understanding of how God operated. God's desire is that we His children know how He operates and can therefore co-labour with Him and expect successful outcomes.

I guess that introduces the aspect of what is a successful outcome. What we see as successful may not be the outcome God truly wants. This is why I stress again it is so imperative that we understand the way God sees things, the way thinks.

Jesus gave us an insight when he said in John 5:19-20

> *"Truly, truly I say to you, the Son can do nothing of Himself, unless it is something He sees the Father doing; for whatever the Father does, these*

things the Son also does in the same way. For the Father loves the Son and shows Him all things that He Himself is doing; and the Father will show Him greater works than these, so that you will be amazed. (NASB)

The exciting thing for us is we also are the sons of God. Once we have made that faith confession and been born again we are adopted into the family of God therefore we are His sons with all the rights of inheritance and expectation of access to our Father.

How do I know that? By Faith! Everything in the kingdom, everything about our relationship with God is by Faith. That is not a cop out - it is real. As we grow in our relationship and understanding of God we can put our Faith to work for the greater things which we can do in His name.

So what happens when we feel we don't have enough Faith? That's the time to realise it is never about us. We are not the saviours, healers or deliverers. He is! If we believe it is us we can fall victim (and probably have fallen victim) to pride. We are privileged to be working with Holy Spirit not instead of Him.

God is not on a coffee break!!

He wants to hear from us - our prayers, our praise, our disappointment, our success and indeed our failure. As we keep this honest line of communication open we grow. We have a deeper knowledge and understanding of Our Heavenly Father and we learn wisdom. The wisdom of heaven not natural wisdom.

I have experienced the good, the bad and the ugly of this Faith walk.

Some years ago my Mother who had loved the Lord all the days of her life had a medical issue and was subsequently diagnosed with a rather sizeable duodenal tumour. The surgeon according to the information he had said she probably would not live through the night and if she did he said she had 36 hours at the most.

I remember stranding the hospital corridor with Paul my husband, my brother and sister in law, holding my hand up in his face declaring that I did not receive that. I felt as though I was caught in whirlwind. My brother was embarrassed by my outburst however, I knew I just had to say it. I was speaking to the spirit realm, not the surgeon, my mothers life was in God's hands and not in the hands of any demonic power.

Suffice to say she lived through the night and she told me the next morning she had been in relentless warfare all night as the enemy tried to snatch her life.

We all prayed, and because of her connections with the body of Christ many people were praying. I rallied every powerful healing minister I knew to pray, come lay hands on her and anoint her.

She went home to be with the Lord at the beginning of the eighth week after the surgery. It was indeed a new beginning. Despite what had been diagnosed she was not in any pain. That in itself was a miracle. She had a private room and with worship and prayer we had created a heavenly atmosphere where angels were always present in that room.

Mum was constantly welcoming nurses and doctors into this place. Every one of them commented on how much they loved being in that room, it was a sanctuary for them. Of course Mum had the opportunity to introduce so many to the love and forgiveness of Christ. The presence of so many of them at her funeral was in itself a testimony of the way she had touched their lives.

I had to come face to face with the fact that the prayers I was praying were selfish and I truly hadn't enquired of the Lord in this particular instance. It wasn't about the Healing power of God, He had not run out of healings. I had failed to understand Mum's will in all this.

I had so much to learn. She was ready to go, the enemy wasn't taking her, The Lord was welcoming her home. She was passing the baton to me to watch over the family in the spirit. After she died I felt a different authority come on me especially in prayer.

At the start of that experience I felt my faith was not strong enough, and the victory which would have seen her come home strong was lost.

God in His lovingkindness showed me she had won. She had no pain, she had finished the race here and passed the baton.

A poignant note to this is that at the moment of her passing, her Bible which had been placed next her head on her pillow and was open to a passage I had been reading over her - fell closed. No one in the room had moved or touched it. She didn't need that word anymore because she was with the Word.

We must believe through situations. That is to say we need a vision of victory and pull that in. In Mum's situation it was my vision which could have completely derailed me. Gods vision was always for victory for us all.

I am reminded of Luke 4:1-13. Jesus was full of the Holy Spirit when He was led into the wilderness by the Spirit of God. He passed the three tests that satan put to Him and indeed left the wilderness in victory.

As we walk this walk of faith we will have victories great and small. It is important not to get proud because of them. Always remember to keep close to the Lord, always watching and always listening to Him.

Verse 13 of that passage is the caution

'And so when the devil had finished every temptation, he left Him until an opportune time.'
Luke 4:13 (NASB)

It stands to reason if satan only departed from Jesus to wait for an opportune time he will do the same with us. Always be at the ready wearing the armour of God and weilding the sword of the Spirit!

My encouragement to each one of us is to endeavour to see each situation from God's perspective. Seek Him and get the prayer strategy from Him. Always trusting in Him for the best outcome for us all.

Your Testimonies

ABOUT THE AUTHOR

Pamela Segneri is the co-founder of Integrity Restoration Ministries Inc and the co-founder and Host of firestartersTV. Her desire is to see you fulfil your God given destiny.

www.integritygroup.org.au

www.firestartersTV.com.au

www.ingramcontent.com/pod-product-compliance
Lightning Source LLC
Chambersburg PA
CBHW050318010526
44107CB00055B/2301